# Table of Contents

I0006447

# The Bitcoin Memoir:

## An Accessible Guide
## to the Blockchain Revolution

*Matt Reid*

*Introducing Bitcoin*:

Hello everyone, I am Bitcoin, the world's first decentralized digital currency. I was launched in 2009 by an unknown person or group using the pseudonym Satoshi Nakamoto. I exist solely in digital form and operate on a decentralized network, which means that no single entity or authority controls me.

My unique technology, called the blockchain, allows me to be transferred securely between users without the need for intermediaries like banks or payment processors. This makes me a popular choice for people who value independence in their financial transactions.

Over the years, my value has grown significantly, and I have become the most well-known and widely-used cryptocurrency in the world. Some people see me as a speculative investment, while others use me for everyday transactions and international money transfers.

If you're interested in learning more about me and my history, this book will provide an in-depth look at how I came to be and what makes me different from traditional forms of currency. Whether you're a seasoned investor or simply curious about the world of cryptocurrency, I invite you to dive into my story and discover what makes me special.

We will delve into my history, including my creation and early adoption, as well as my evolution and growth over the years. We will explore my myriad features and how they differentiate me from traditional currencies, as well as my potential applications beyond finance.

We will also address some of the controversies surrounding me and examine both the potential benefits and risks associated with using me as a means of payment and investment.

Overall, this book will provide readers with a deep understanding of who I am, what I represent, where I came from, when I first emerged, and why I matter in the world of finance and technology. If you are a Bitcoin beginner or just want to hear my story, this book is a must-read for anyone interested in understanding 'the Internet of Money', providing a comprehensive overview of my groundbreaking technology!

*Chapter 1*:
Bitcoin vs Dollar Dynamics [BTC v USD]

Bitcoin and the US dollar differ in several ways, including their monetary policies and supply dynamics.

Firstly, Bitcoin is a decentralized digital currency that operates on a peer-to-peer network. It was designed to have a limited supply of 21 million coins, which are slowly released into circulation through a process called 'mining'. This means that the supply of Bitcoin is strictly limited, and the rate of its release is predetermined by its protocol. This fixed supply makes Bitcoin a deflationary currency, where its value tends to increase over time due to scarcity.

On the other hand, the US dollar is a fiat currency, meaning that its value is not backed by any physical commodity but is instead derived from the faith and credit of the US government. The Federal Reserve, which operates as a public-private partnership, acts as the central bank of the United States, and has the power to influence the supply of dollars by adjusting interest rates and by printing more money.

The Federal Reserve can set interest rates to influence borrowing, lending, and spending within the economy. When interest rates are low, borrowing becomes cheaper, and people are more likely to take out loans to invest in businesses or make large purchases. This can manually stimulate economic growth but can also lead to inflation if too much money is borrowed and spent.

Additionally, the Federal Reserve has the power to print more money, which can increase the supply of dollars in circulation. However, this can also lead to inflation if too much money is printed relative to the available goods and services in the economy.

Bitcoin's manufactured scarcity is designed to ensure that its supply is limited and deflationary, while the US dollar's supply is managed by the Federal Reserve through interest rate adjustments and money printing.

Money may not grow on trees, however its creation is conjured onto cotton and linen with the stroke of a printing press. This process manifests power and counterfeits precariously positioned fortunes, bolstered by tarnished decree, like a palace of cards.

*Chapter 2*:
*Who* is Bitcoin?

I am Bitcoin, a digital currency that was created in 2009 by an unknown person or group using the pseudonym Satoshi Nakamoto. My origin story is shrouded in mystery, and my creator's identity remains a mystery to this day. But what is clear is that I am a revolutionary.

Unlike traditional currencies that are backed by governments, I am decentralized and operate on a peer-to-peer network. This means that I am not controlled by any central authority and can be sent from person to person without the need for intermediaries like banks.

My popularity has grown rapidly over the years, and I am now accepted by merchants and businesses all over the world. Some people buy me as an investment, hoping that my value will increase over time, while others use me as a means of payment for goods and services.

One of my unique features is my limited supply. Only 21 million of me will ever exist, and as of May 2023, around 19.3 million of me have already been mined. The process of mining me involves using powerful computers to solve complex mathematical problems, and the miners who successfully solve these problems are rewarded with newly created *me*.

But I am not without my controversies. Some people criticize me for my association with illegal activities like money laundering and drug trafficking, while others argue that my volatility makes me too risky for mainstream adoption.

I am compelled to note that the use of cryptocurrencies for criminal activity is often overstated. In fact, according to Chainalysis' 2021 report, criminal activity represented only a small fraction of all cryptocurrency transactions. In 2019, criminal activity accounted for 2.1% of cryptocurrency transaction volume worldwide, equivalent to approximately $21.4 billion worth of transfers. This figure decreased significantly in 2020, with criminal activity making up just 0.34% ($10.0 billion) of all cryptocurrency activity.

To put this in perspective, the UN estimates that between 2% and 5% of the global GDP ($1.6 to $4 trillion) is annually connected to money laundering and illicit activity. Therefore, criminal activity using crypto is much smaller than fiat currency, and its use is declining year by year.

Despite these misconceptions and criticisms, I have gained mainstream acceptance as a legitimate asset and I am traded on numerous cryptocurrency exchanges worldwide. Since my inception, I have continued to grow in popularity and importance, but this trend has been far from a straight line. I have acted much differently than other monetary options, and some people cannot stomach my volatility. Although, my volatility has lessened as I have matured. I believe my technology, the blockchain, has the potential to revolutionize industries beyond finance—such as smart contracts and democracy on the blockchain.

*Chapter 3*:
*What* is Bitcoin?

I am Digital Cash that exists in a decentralized ecosystem, supporting a peer-to-peer network with the purpose to hold and exchange value online. Unlike traditional currencies that are backed by governments, I am not controlled by any central authority, and my transactions are recorded on a public ledger called the blockchain that no one can tamper with thanks to the 256-bit SHA hash functions that ensure my military-level security.

At my core, I am a set of computer code that was designed to be a decentralized, trustless, permissionless, and secure way to transfer value online. I am not physical money, but rather a digital representation of value that can be sent from one person to another without the need for intermediaries like banks.

❖ Decentralized: Decentralized refers to a system or network in which decision-making and control are distributed across multiple nodes or participants, rather than being centralized in a single authority or entity. In a decentralized system, there is no central point of control or failure, which can make the system more resilient, secure, and transparent.

In regards to blockchain, transactions are validated and recorded by a network of nodes rather than a single central authority, which makes them resistant to censorship, fraud, and hacking. Decentralization can also facilitate peer-to-peer transactions, the creation of decentralized applications, and opens the world to novel financial vehicles, providing new opportunities for innovation and collaboration.

❖    Trustless: Trustless is a term used to describe a system or transaction in which parties can interact with each other and exchange value without the need for trust or intermediaries.

In a trustless system, transactions are facilitated by cryptographic protocols and smart contracts that are programmed to execute automatically based on predefined rules. This eliminates the need for intermediaries such as banks, lawyers, or other trusted third parties to oversee the transaction, and the need for parties to rely on each other's good faith.

The term "trustless" can be somewhat misleading, as it does not mean that trust is completely eliminated from the transaction. Instead, it means that trust is minimized, and parties can transact with each other based on the predefined rules and protocols of the system, rather than relying on trust in an intermediary or counterparty.

❖ Permissionless: Permissionless refers to a system or network that allows anyone to participate, transact, and interact with others in the network without needing permission or approval from a central authority or gatekeeper.

The term "permissionless" should not be confused with "anonymous," as permissionless systems can still require users to identify themselves and adhere to certain rules and protocols. However, permissionless systems allow anyone to participate on an equal footing, regardless of their identity or background.

❖ Secure: Bitcoin uses several key technologies to ensure its security, including: Cryptography, Blockchain, Proof-of-Work, and Decentralization.

A. Cryptography: Bitcoin relies on cryptographic techniques to secure its transactions and prevent fraud. This includes the use of public-key cryptography to create digital signatures, which are used to verify the authenticity of transactions.

B. Blockchain: The blockchain is a distributed ledger that records all Bitcoin transactions in a secure, permanent, and tamper-proof manner. The blockchain is maintained by a network of nodes, and each node has a copy of the entire blockchain, which ensures that there is no central point of failure or control. Each block on the blockchain contains a set of transactions, and once a block is added to the chain, it cannot be altered.

C. Proof-of-Work: Bitcoin uses a consensus algorithm known as Proof-of-Work (PoW) to validate transactions and add new blocks to the blockchain. PoW requires nodes to solve complex mathematical puzzles in order to validate transactions and earn rewards. This system ensures that nodes are incentivized to act honestly and validate transactions accurately.

Overall, the combination of cryptography, blockchain technology, PoW consensus, and decentralization makes Bitcoin a secure and reliable network for transacting and storing value. However, as with any technology, there are still potential vulnerabilities and security risks. Ongoing development and improvement is necessary to ensure the continued security and reliability of the Bitcoin network.

Some consider me 'digital gold'. Others say I am the infrastructure of a financial renaissance.

*Chapter 4*:
*When* Was Bitcoin Born?

Bitcoin, the world's first decentralized digital currency, was born on January 3, 2009. It was created by an unknown person or group of people using the pseudonym "Satoshi Nakamoto."

Nakamoto's invention came after years of research and experimentation in the field of cryptography and digital currencies. The goal was to create a peer-to-peer electronic cash system that would be free from the control of governments and financial institutions.

The idea of digital cash had been around since the 1980s, but it was not until the invention of blockchain technology that it became possible to create a secure and decentralized system.

Bitcoin was the first application of blockchain technology, and it quickly gained popularity among those who saw it as a way to bypass the traditional banking system. In the early days, bitcoin was primarily used for online purchases, but as more merchants began accepting it, its value began to rise.

The first bitcoin transaction took place between Nakamoto and a programmer named Hal Finney. Nakamoto sent Finney

10 bitcoins, which at the time were worth virtually nothing. Today, that same transaction would be worth a quarter of $1 million.

Over the years, many people have tried to uncover the identity of Satoshi Nakamoto, but to this day, no one knows for sure who he, she, or they are. Nakamoto disappeared from the public eye in 2011, leaving the development of Bitcoin to a community of volunteers.

Since its inception, Bitcoin has gone through many ups and downs. Its value has fluctuated wildly, and it has been subject to numerous hacks and scams, but persevered. Bitcoin continues to thrive, and its underlying technology, the blockchain, is being hailed as a game-changer that is helping to scale an increasingly high-tech society.

*Cyberpunks & The Byzantine Generals Problem*:

The Byzantine Generals Problem is a computer science problem that relates to distributed systems and communication protocols. It was first introduced in a 1982 paper titled "The Byzantine Generals Problem" by Leslie Lamport, Robert Shostak, and Marshall Pease.

The problem is named after the historical Byzantine army, which faced a similar problem when trying to coordinate their actions during a military campaign. In the computer science version of the problem, a group of generals are trying to coordinate their actions to either attack or retreat from an enemy, but some of the generals may be traitors who will intentionally send false messages to confuse the others.

The challenge is to develop a protocol that allows the loyal generals to reach a consensus on a plan of action despite the presence of traitors who may try to disrupt the process by sending false or conflicting messages. The problem is important because it models situations where distributed systems need to reach a consensus in the presence of faulty or malicious components.

Solutions to the Byzantine Generals Problem have practical applications in fields such as cryptography, distributed computing, and blockchain technology.

Cyberpunk is a subgenre of science fiction that emerged in the 1980s. It often explores dystopian futures where central powers use technology to betray society, leading to a breakdown of trust and a rise in individualism.

It is possible that the ideas and themes explored in cyberpunk literature and movies may have influenced the development of Bitcoin and other cryptocurrencies. The cyberpunk genre often features themes such as decentralization, anonymity, and anti-authoritarianism, which are also key features of Bitcoin.

Additionally, the concept of electronic cash, which was a key component of Satoshi Nakamoto's original Bitcoin white paper, has been explored in science fiction literature for decades before Bitcoin's invention. For example, Neal Stephenson's novel "Snow Crash" features a digital currency called "Kongbucks," which shares some similarities with Bitcoin.

One of the defining characteristics of 'cyberpunk' is its focus on the impact of technology on society, particularly on the marginalized and disempowered. In many cyberpunk stories, corporations and governments use advanced technology to exert control over the population and maintain their power, often at the expense of individual freedom and privacy.

These dystopian futures often involve scenarios where advanced technologies such as artificial intelligence, virtual reality, and cybernetic enhancements have become integral parts of society, but have also led to a breakdown of trust and a rise in inequality. This can lead to themes such as corporate domination, government surveillance, and cybercrime, which are all common in cyberpunk literature and media.

*Chapter 5*:
*Where* is Bitcoin?

Hello again, it's me Bitcoin, a currency that exists entirely on the internet. I do not have a physical form like traditional currencies, so I cannot be held or stored in a traditional wallet or bank account. Instead, I am represented by a unique set of code that exists on the blockchain, a public ledger that records all transactions involving me.

I am stored in digital wallets, which can be accessed from any device with an internet connection. These wallets can be hosted on online exchanges, which allow people to buy and sell me for other currencies, or they can be hosted on personal devices like computers or smartphones.

As a digital currency, I am accepted by merchants and businesses all over the world. Some online retailers and service providers, like Microsoft and Expedia, accept me as payment for their goods and services. In El Salvador, I am even recognized as legal tender alongside their national currency.

Several other countries, including Ukraine, Panama, and Brazil, have discussed or considered the possibility of legalizing or regulating cryptocurrencies, but they have not yet adopted them as legal tender.

In the United States, the state of Wyoming has passed laws recognizing cryptocurrencies as legal property, and Miami, Florida, has launched its own cryptocurrency, MiamiCoin, as a means of fundraising for the city. However, cryptocurrencies are not yet legal tender in the United States, and their status as property means that they are subject to capital gains tax when sold or exchanged for other assets.

It's worth noting that the legal status of cryptocurrencies can vary widely from country to country and can change as regulators and policymakers adapt to the evolving landscape of cryptocurrencies and blockchain technology. Some areas are more open to my use than others. In countries with unstable currencies or limited access to traditional banking services, I am often seen as a viable alternative for people who want to store value or transfer money without relying on traditional financial systems.

The IRS has allowed US citizens to pay their taxes with Bitcoin since 2014. In a guidance notice issued that year, the IRS stated that virtual currencies, including Bitcoin, are treated as property for federal tax purposes.

The guidance also clarified that taxpayers can use virtual currencies to pay their taxes as long as the virtual currency is valued at its fair market value at the time of payment. Taxpayers must report the fair market value of the virtual currency on their tax returns.

It's worth noting that while the IRS allows taxpayers to pay their taxes with Bitcoin, it's not a commonly used method of payment. Many taxpayers are hesitant to use Bitcoin to pay their taxes due to its volatility and the potential tax implications of using it to make a payment.

Overall, my digital nature allows me to exist and be used anywhere in the world with an internet connection. While my acceptance and popularity may vary by region, I continue to grow in importance and relevance as a digital asset with the potential to revolutionize the way we think about money and value.

*Metaverse, NFTs, & Play-to-Earn Games*:

There is a strong link between blockchain technology, the metaverse, and play-to-earn games.

Bitcoin's Blockchain technology can play a significant role in enabling the metaverse. Here are some ways in which blockchain can facilitate the development of the metaverse:

1.      Decentralized finance (DeFi) - Bitcoin's underlying technology, blockchain, can enable decentralized finance, which allows for the creation of decentralized financial applications that can be used within the metaverse. These DeFi applications can include lending, borrowing, and trading of virtual currencies, assets, and commodities.

2.      NFTs - Non-fungible tokens (NFTs) are unique digital assets that are stored on a blockchain. Bitcoin's blockchain can be used to create and store NFTs that can be used within the metaverse for things like virtual real estate, avatars, virtual goods, and virtual experiences.

3.      Interoperability - Bitcoin's blockchain can serve as a bridge between different metaverse platforms, enabling interoperability and the seamless transfer of assets and currencies between different metaverse environments.

4.      Smart Contracts - Smart contracts are self-executing contracts with the terms of the agreement

between buyer and seller being directly written into lines of code. Smart contracts can be used to automate the exchange of virtual or physical goods and services, both in the metaverse and down here on Earth.

By using blockchain technology, the metaverse can create new robust economic models and enable users to have true ownership and control over their digital assets. Blockchain technology is particularly important in the context of the metaverse and play-to-earn games. The metaverse is essentially a virtual world where users can interact with each other and digital assets in a shared space, and blockchain technology can help ensure the security and ownership of these assets.

In play-to-earn games, players are rewarded with cryptocurrency or digital assets for completing in-game tasks or challenges. These rewards are typically stored on the blockchain and can be traded or sold outside of the game.

The metaverse and play-to-earn games also enable new business models and revenue streams for creators and developers. With blockchain technology, creators can sell digital assets and content directly to users, without intermediaries taking a cut.

Overall, blockchain technology is a key enabler for the metaverse, virtual property (NFTs), and play-to-earn games, as it provides a secure and transparent way to manage digital assets and transactions. As these industries continue to grow, it's likely that we will see even more innovative use cases for blockchain technology in the future.

*Chapter 6*:
*How* Does Bitcoin Work?

Understanding how I work can be a bit complex, but I will do my best to explain it in simple terms.

At my core, I am a set of computer code that exists on a decentralized network of computers called the blockchain. The blockchain is a public ledger that records all transactions involving me, and it is maintained by a network of users around the world.

When someone wants to send me to someone else, they create a transaction and broadcast it to the network. This transaction contains information about the sender, the recipient, and the amount of me being sent.

The network then verifies and validates this transaction using complex mathematical algorithms, and once it is confirmed, the transaction is added to a block on the blockchain. This block is then added to the chain of blocks, forming a permanent and unalterable record of the transaction.

This process of validation is known as mining, and it is the way new units of me are created and added to the network. Miners use powerful computers to solve complex equations and through consensus verify transactions. When miners verify a transaction properly they are rewarded with newly created units of Bitcoin (BTC) for their efforts.

One of my key features is my limited supply, with only 21 million units of me set to ever exist. The process of mining becomes increasingly difficult over time, and the reward for successful mining is reduced every four years in a process known as halving. This is done to ensure that I am not subject to inflation and that my value is maintained over time.

Bitcoin uses the SHA-256 (Secure Hash Algorithm 256-bit) hashing algorithm to secure its blockchain. The SHA-256 algorithm is a widely used cryptographic hash function that generates a fixed-size 256-bit (32-byte) hash value. It is designed by the United States National Security Agency (NSA) and is considered to be a secure hashing algorithm that is resistant to collision attacks.

In the Bitcoin network, the SHA-256 algorithm is used to generate the digital signature for each transaction and to secure the blockchain by mining new blocks. Miners compete to solve a complex mathematical problem using the SHA-256 algorithm, and the first one to find a solution that meets the network's difficulty requirements gets to add a new block to the blockchain and receive a reward in Bitcoin. The SHA-256 algorithm is an integral part of Bitcoin's security model and has been proven to be reliable and effective in practice.

*In order to participate, you need a Bitcoin wallet:*

Bitcoin wallets are software applications that allow you to store, send, and receive Bitcoin. They essentially function as a digital wallet, sort of like a physical wallet holding your cash and cards except digitally archived into the blockchain. Bitcoin wallets come in various forms, including desktop, mobile, hardware, and web-based wallets.

• Desktop wallets are software programs that you download and install on your computer.

There are several Bitcoin desktop wallets available. Here are a few examples:

1. Electrum - This is a popular Bitcoin wallet that is available for Windows, Mac, and Linux. It offers a range of features, including support for hardware wallets, multi-signature transactions, and two-factor authentication.

2. Exodus - This is a desktop wallet that supports multiple cryptocurrencies, including Bitcoin. It has a

user-friendly interface and offers features such as a built-in exchange and portfolio tracker.

3.      Armory - This is an advanced Bitcoin wallet that is designed for users who require high-level security. It is available for Windows, Mac, and Linux and offers features such as cold storage and multi-signature transactions.

4.      Bitcoin Core - This is the official Bitcoin desktop wallet and is available for Windows, Mac, and Linux. It is a full node wallet, which means that it downloads and stores the entire Bitcoin blockchain.

5.      Atomic Wallet - This is a desktop wallet that supports multiple cryptocurrencies, including Bitcoin. It offers a range of features such as staking, atomic swaps, and built-in exchange. It is available for Windows, Mac, and Linux.

•      Mobile wallets are apps that you can download to your smartphone or tablet. They are convenient because you can use them on the go, but they are considered less secure than desktop wallets because they are susceptible to hacking. Examples of mobile wallets include Mycelium, BRD, and Trust.

Trust Wallet is good for beginners and beyond. It is a popular mobile cryptocurrency wallet that supports various cryptocurrencies, including Bitcoin. It is developed by Binance, one of the largest cryptocurrency exchanges in the world.

Trust Wallet is generally considered to be a good Bitcoin wallet, as it offers a high level of security and ease of use. It uses advanced security features, such as encryption and biometric authentication, to keep your private keys and funds safe.

Additionally, Trust Wallet is a non-custodial wallet, meaning you have full control over your funds and private keys. This is important because it reduces the risk of your funds being lost or stolen due to the actions of a third-party custodian.

Overall, if you're looking for a reliable and secure mobile Bitcoin wallet, Trust Wallet is definitely worth considering. However, as with any financial application, it's important to do your own research and due diligence before entrusting your funds to any wallet.

- Hardware wallets are physical devices that you can connect to your computer or smartphone via USB. They are marketed as offering the highest level of security because they store your private keys offline. However, they still require some trust. It is important to fully research the product and make sure to purchase directly from the manufacturer to avoid third-party tampering.

- Web-based wallets are online services that allow you to store your Bitcoin online. They are considered less secure than other types of wallets because they are vulnerable to hacking and phishing attacks. Examples of web-based wallets include Coinbase, Binance, and Bittrex.

When choosing a Bitcoin wallet, it's important to consider factors such as security, ease of use, and compatibility with your devices. You should also research the reputation of the wallet provider and read reviews from other users.

To acquire Bitcoin before sending it to your personal private wallet, you can follow these steps on Coinbase or Cash App:

On Coinbase:

1.      Sign in to your Coinbase account and navigate to the Buy/Sell page.

2.      Select Bitcoin as the cryptocurrency you want to buy and enter the amount you want to purchase.

3.      Choose the payment method you want to use and complete the transaction.

4.      Once your purchase is complete, your Bitcoin will be available in your Coinbase account (in some cases, transactions may be pending for a few days before funds can be sent.)

5.      Navigate to the "Accounts" tab and select your Bitcoin wallet.

6.      Click on "Send" and enter the address of your personal private wallet.

7.      Confirm the details and click "Send" again to transfer the Bitcoin to your personal wallet.

On Cash App:

1.      Sign in to your Cash App account and navigate to the "Investing" tab.

2.      Select Bitcoin as the investment option and enter the amount you want to purchase.

3.      Choose the payment method you want to use and complete the transaction.

4.      Once your purchase is complete, your Bitcoin will be available in your Cash App account.

5.      Navigate to the "Withdraw Bitcoin" tab and select the amount of Bitcoin you want to transfer to your personal private wallet.

6.      Enter the address of your personal private wallet and confirm the details.

7.      Click "Confirm" to transfer the Bitcoin to your personal wallet.

It's important to note that both Coinbase and Cash App charge fees for buying and transferring Bitcoin. Make sure to check the fees and transaction limits before making any transactions. Additionally, always double-check the 'receive' address of your personal wallet before sending any Bitcoin to ensure that you don't accidentally send it to the wrong address.

The terms "hot" and "cold" are used to describe the different types of cryptocurrency wallets based on their connectivity to the internet.

1.      Hot Wallet: A hot wallet is a wallet that is connected to the internet and is therefore more vulnerable

to hacking or other security threats. Hot wallets include online wallets or software wallets that are installed on a computer or mobile device.

2.      Cold Wallet: A cold wallet is a wallet that is not connected to the internet and is therefore more secure from hacking and other security threats. Cold wallets include hardware wallets like Trezor, Tangem, and Arculus, which are physical devices that store your private keys offline.

There is also a type of cold wallet called a "paper wallet". This type of wallet is printed onto paper and should be laminated and stored somewhere safe like a fireproof vault and/or safety deposit box. Paper wallets can provide a high level of security, but they also come with certain risks and considerations. Paper wallets are vulnerable to physical damage, human error, and they require some technical knowledge and a careful understanding of the process to ensure the generation of secure keys and the proper handling and storage of the wallet. It's essential to follow best practices. It's also important to create multiple copies of the paper wallet and store them in separate secure locations. This ensures that if one copy is lost, damaged, or inaccessible, you still have backups available. When properly executed, paper wallets offer the advantage of offline storage, reducing the risk of online attacks or hacking attempts. This can be a viable option for long-term Bitcoin storage.

In general, hot wallets are more convenient for frequent transactions, while cold wallets are more secure for long-term storage of cryptocurrency. Ultimately, the choice of wallet depends on an individual's specific needs and preferences for security and ease of use.

*Chapter 7*:
*Why* is Bitcoin Important?

I am Bitcoin, a digital currency that has piqued the interest of humanity. But why am I important, and why should you care about me? In this chapter, we will explore the various reasons why I am relevant and significant in today's world.

❖      Decentralization and Transparency: One of my key features is that I operate on a decentralized network, meaning that I am not controlled by any single authority or institution. This also means that all transactions involving me are transparent and publicly visible on the blockchain, allowing for greater accountability and trust.

❖      Security: Because I operate on a decentralized network, I am highly secure and resistant to hacking or fraud. My cryptographic protocols and consensus mechanisms ensure that all transactions involving me are valid and cannot be tampered with.

❖      Inflation Resistance: With a limited supply of only 21 million units of me, I am designed to be resistant to inflation and maintain my value over time. This makes me a popular choice for individuals and businesses looking to store value and protect their assets from inflation.

❖ Borderless Transactions: As a digital currency, I can be sent and received anywhere in the world with an internet connection. This allows for independently executed fast and efficient cross-border transactions.

❖ Financial Inclusion: In many parts of the world, traditional banking services are not widely available or accessible. As digital cash, I offer a viable alternative for people looking to store value or transfer money without relying on traditional financial institutions.

❖ Investment Opportunities: My unique and multifaceted appeal and limited collectible nature has made me a popular choice for investors looking to diversify their portfolios. Many people believe that I have the potential to become a major asset class in the future.

*Kryptonite for Fractional Reserve Banking Scheme*:

In the event of a run on banks, Bitcoin may be more reliable than getting cash because of fractional reserve banking.

Fractional reserve banking is a banking system where only a fraction of total deposits are held in reserve, while the rest are loaned out or invested in other assets. This means that if too many people try to withdraw their money at the same time, the bank may not have enough reserves to meet all the demands for cash.

Bitcoin, on the other hand, is not subject to fractional reserve banking, as it is not programmed to be such a scheme. Users can access and use their Bitcoin at will without relying on financial institutions.

However, it is important to note that Bitcoin's value is highly volatile, and it may not be a stable store of value in times of crisis or uncertainty. Additionally, Bitcoin may not be accepted as widely as cash yet, and there may be limitations on its use in certain countries or regions.

Whether you are looking for a secure way to store value, make cross-border transactions, or invest in the future, I offer a compelling option. However, it is important to carefully consider the risks and limitations associated with Bitcoin before relying on it as a store of value or medium of exchange.

*Chapter 8*:
Fun Facts & Quotes About Bitcoin

I am Bitcoin, a digital currency that has captured the world's attention. While I am serious business, here are some fun facts about me that you may not have known:

1.      The First Purchase Made with Bitcoin: On May 22, 2010, a programmer named Laszlo Hanyecz purchased two pizzas for 10,000 Bitcoins. At the time, the Bitcoins were worth around $41. Today, those same Bitcoins would be worth over $250 million!

2.      Satoshi Nakamoto: The mysterious founder of Bitcoin, Satoshi Nakamoto, is still unknown. It is believed that Nakamoto is a pseudonym for the person or group of people who created Bitcoin. To this day, their identity remains a mystery.

3.      Lost Bitcoins: It is estimated that around 20% of all Bitcoins are lost or inaccessible, which equates to around 4 million Bitcoins worth over $100 billion at today's prices.

4.      Bitcoin Mining Energy Consumption: The process of mining Bitcoin requires a lot of computing power and

energy. In fact, it is estimated that the annual energy consumption of Bitcoin mining is more than the entire country of Argentina! To put that into perspective, a recent report from Galaxy Digital found that both banking systems and gold exchanges worldwide consumed more than twice that of Bitcoin's energy consumption. That means Bitcoin is 'greener' than fiat and gold.

5.      Bitcoin ATMs: As of 2021, there are over 20,000 Bitcoin ATMs located in more than 70 countries around the world. These ATMs allow users to buy and sell Bitcoin using cash or debit cards.

6.      The First Bitcoin Billionaire: In 2017, Tyler and Cameron Winklevoss, who famously sued Mark Zuckerberg over the creation of Facebook, became the first Bitcoin billionaires. They had invested $11 million in Bitcoin back in 2013, which had grown to be worth over $1 billion by 2017.

7.      Bitcoin as a Payment Method: While still not widely accepted, many major companies now accept Bitcoin as a payment method, including Microsoft, AT&T, and Overstock.com.

8.      Bitcoin in Space: Several blockchain firms have made significant advancements in bringing Bitcoin (BTC) and other cryptocurrencies to space. Blockstream Satellite has launched a network of six satellites in geosynchronous orbit that broadcast Bitcoin's blockchain globally, allowing anyone to receive blockchain data anywhere in the world, anytime. Thanks to Blockstream's network of satellites, the entire Bitcoin blockchain is beamed to Earth without the need for an internet connection, making Bitcoin truly decentralized and resistant to censorship and outages caused by natural disasters or other earthbound circumstances. SpaceChain, a blockchain-powered space-as-a-service company, has launched an Ethereum-enabled payload that was installed at the International Space Station, enabling private companies and individuals worldwide to launch products with use cases beyond monetary. These advancements suggest that the use of blockchain and cryptocurrencies in space is likely to expand in the future.

These are just a few fun facts about me, Bitcoin. As I continue to grow and evolve, I am sure that there will be many more interesting and exciting developments to come.

Here are some notable quotes about Bitcoin:

- *"Bitcoin is a remarkable cryptographic achievement and the ability to create something which is not duplicable in the digital world has enormous value..." —Eric Schmidt, former CEO of Google*

- *"Bitcoin is a technological tour de force." —Bill Gates, co-founder of Microsoft*

- *"Even though I'm a pro-crypto, pro-Bitcoin maximalist...I do wonder whether at this point, Bitcoin should also be thought of in part as a Chinese financial weapon against the U.S." —Peter Thiel, co-founder of PayPal*

- *"It's money 2.0, a huge huge huge deal." —Chamath Palihapitiya, previous head of AOL instant messenger*

- *"Between 2008-22, the Fed partnered with a handful of big banks to print $10 trillion — ten centuries of wealth in 15 years — a bonanza for the Banksters...Cryptocurrencies like Bitcoin give the public an escape route from the splatter zone when this bubble invariably bursts. So the White House is colluding with the banksters to keep us all trapped in the bubble of profiteering and control." —Robert F. Kennedy Jr.*

- *"It's gold for nerds." —Stephen Colbert, Comedian*

- *"Bitcoin is a very exciting development, it might lead to a world currency. I think over the next decade it will grow to become one of the most important ways to pay for things and transfer assets." —Kim Dotcom, entrepreneur and internet activist*

- *"At the end of the day, bitcoin is programmable money. When you have programmable money, the possibilities are truly endless. We can take many of the basic concepts of the current system that depend on legal contracts, and we can convert these into algorithmic contracts, into mathematical transactions that can be enforced on the bitcoin network. As I've said, there is no third party, there is no counterparty. If I choose to send value from one part of the network to another, it is peer-to-peer with no one in between. If I invent a new form of money, I can deploy it to the entire world and invite others to come and join me. Bitcoin is not just money for the internet. Yes, it's perfect money for the internet. It's instant, it's safe, it's free. Yes, it is money for the internet, but it's so much more. Bitcoin is the internet of money. Currency is only the first application. If you grasp that, you can look beyond the price, you can look beyond the volatility, you can look beyond the fad. At its core, bitcoin is a revolutionary technology that will change the world forever." —Andreas Antonopoulos, author and Bitcoin advocate*

- *"I'm still bullish on bitcoin ... Bitcoin is not the same as Sam Bankman-Fried. It's not bitcoin, it's FTX that's the problem." —Robert Kiyosaki, the author of "Rich Dad Poor Dad"*

- *"The root problem with conventional currency is all the trust that's required to make it work. The central bank must be trusted not to debase the currency, but the history of fiat currencies is full of breaches of that trust. Banks must be trusted to hold our money and transfer it electronically, but they lend it out in waves of credit bubbles with barely a fraction in reserve." —Satoshi Nakamoto*

- *"There are 3 eras of currency: Commodity based, politically based, and now, math based." —Chris Dixon, General Partner of Andreessen Horowitz*

- *"Bitcoin is the currency of resistance." —Max Keiser, host of The Keiser Report*

- *"...crypto is a far better way to transfer values than a piece of paper..." —Elon Musk*

- *"I personally think that Bitcoin is worthless." —Jamie Diamond, CEO of JPMorgan Chase & Co.*

## Chapter 9:
## Quantum Computing/Long-Term Viability Considerations

*Is Bitcoin Quantum Resistant?*

Bitcoin, like most existing cryptocurrencies, is not currently quantum resistant. This means that it is theoretically vulnerable to being hacked by a quantum computer in the future.

Quantum computers are a type of computer that uses quantum mechanics to perform certain types of calculations much faster than classical computers. This includes calculations that are required to break the cryptographic algorithms that secure Bitcoin transactions.

However, the threat of quantum computers to Bitcoin is not imminent. The technology for building large-scale quantum computers is still in its infancy, and it is not yet clear when or if such computers will become widely available.

That being said, there are efforts underway to make Bitcoin and other cryptocurrencies quantum-resistant by developing new cryptographic algorithms that are more resistant to quantum attacks. These efforts include the development of post-quantum cryptography (PQC) standards that could replace the current cryptographic algorithms used in Bitcoin. One proposal is to switch to a PQC scheme, such as the hash-based signature scheme known as the Lamport signature. Another proposal is to use a hybrid system that combines classical and quantum-resistant encryption.

Bitcoin's current encryption scheme, the Elliptic Curve Digital Signature Algorithm (ECDSA), is not quantum computing resistant. This means that if a sufficiently powerful quantum computer were to be built, it could potentially break the security of Bitcoin transactions and steal funds.

However, it's important to note that building a quantum computer capable of breaking Bitcoin's encryption is still a very challenging task. While there has been progress in developing quantum computers, they are still in their early stages and nowhere near powerful enough to pose a threat to Bitcoin's security.

In regards to traditional finance, it is theoretically possible that a sufficiently powerful quantum computer could be used to break the encryption that currently protects many bank accounts and financial systems.

To mitigate this risk, many financial institutions and governments are already working to develop and implement new cryptographic algorithms that are designed to be quantum-resistant.

Additionally, financial institutions and governments are also exploring other security measures, such as multi-factor authentication and biometric identification, to help secure bank accounts and other financial systems against potential threats from quantum computing and other advanced technologies.

*Could the Internet ever shut down and how would that affect assets held in traditional financial institutions compared to Bitcoin?*

Yes, the Internet could potentially be shut down in certain regions or countries, although it would be difficult to shut down the entire global Internet. In the event of an Internet shutdown, the Bitcoin network would also be affected, as it relies on the Internet to operate.

However, even if the Internet was shut down temporarily, the Bitcoin network would not necessarily be permanently damaged. Bitcoin transactions are stored on a decentralized ledger called the blockchain, which is maintained by a network of nodes around the world. These nodes would continue to operate and record transactions even if the Internet was down, as long as they were able to communicate with each other through alternative means, such as satellite or mesh networks.

In terms of comparing the impact on Bitcoin versus traditional bank accounts, the effect would likely be less severe for Bitcoin. Traditional bank accounts rely heavily on online access to process transactions, and an Internet shutdown would severely limit their ability to function. However, with Bitcoin, transactions can still be processed and recorded even if the Internet is down for a short period of time.

If the Internet was shut down for an extended period of time, it would be difficult to process new transactions, but the existing records on the blockchain would still be saved. When the Internet was powered back up, it would be possible to resume transactions and add new blocks to the blockchain.

*Would the United States of America Ever Ban Bitcoin?*

It is impossible to say with certainty whether the United States government would ever ban Bitcoin, but I believe that is of low probability.

While there have been discussions and debates in the US government and regulatory bodies about how to regulate Bitcoin and other cryptocurrencies, no ban has been put in place. In fact, some government officials have expressed support for Bitcoin and its potential benefits, while others have expressed concerns about its potential risks.

It is important to note that banning Bitcoin outright would likely be a challenging and complex undertaking, given the decentralized nature of the cryptocurrency and its global reach. Additionally, a ban on Bitcoin would likely face opposition from those who view it as a legitimate form of payment and investment, and many Americans would continue to hold their BTC offshore.

If the US were to ban Bitcoin, it could be seen by some as a sign of weakness in the fiat system, as it would suggest that the government feels threatened by the rise of an alternative currency. If the government banned Bitcoin, that action would likely be blamed on illegitimate concerns regarding money laundering, tax evasion, and other illegal activities that have been facilitated by cryptocurrencies. This scapegoating would be illegitimate because the dollar is known for complicity in most transactions of illicit activity, not Bitcoin or crypto. Authoritarians would use every excuse that incites fear since it is their most successful tool to steer public opinion. However, Bitcoin enables full transparency and transactions are not necessarily anonymous, so there would be no acceptable reason to ban BTC.

A ban on Bitcoin could be seen as an authoritarian attempt by the government to assert control over the financial system and limit individual freedoms. Any government who seeks to ban or overregulate Bitcoin would be acting tyrannically and would show that they are not very inclusive and do not value diversity of choice. This would be seen as a desperate attempt for oligarchs, banking cartels, crony corporatists, and totalitarian statists to maintain hegemony as my technology renders their unjust system obsolete... but I am biased.

*Chapter 10:*
Central Bank Digital Currency

CBDCs are digital versions of traditional fiat currencies (e.g., the US dollar, Euro, etc.) that are issued and controlled by central banks, such as the Federal Reserve in the US or the European Central Bank in Europe.

CBDCs differ from Bitcoin and other cryptocurrencies in several ways. First, CBDCs are centralized and issued by a government or central bank, whereas cryptocurrencies like Bitcoin are decentralized and not controlled by any single entity. Second, CBDCs are designed to be legal tender and used for everyday transactions, similar to physical cash, whereas cryptocurrencies are often used more for investment purposes or as a store of value. Third, CBDCs are likely to be subject to government regulations and restrictions, while cryptocurrencies are typically designed to be free from government control.

CBDCs could potentially make transactions faster and more efficient. But trading convenience for freedom is not for everyone. After expressing concern over not knowing who is using cash bills, the Bank of International Settlements (BIS) stated recently that the "central bank will have absolute control on the rules and regulations that will determine the use of [CBDCs]...and also we will have the technology to enforce that." Some financial experts have expressed concerns for this use of government programmable money that can be issued based on compliance of eccentric and excessive edicts that are based on partisan ideology—and if tied to a social credit score, this type of high-tech government fiat could limit certain purchases that contribute to over consumption of carbon credits allowed on the platform, for example. CBDCs could also help governments monitor and regulate the economy more effectively by providing real-time data on the flow of money.

Overall, CBDCs and Bitcoin are two different types of digital currencies with opposing purposes. While CBDCs are designed to be a digital version of traditional fiat currencies issued and controlled by central banks, Bitcoin was designed to be free from government control.

Several countries have already implemented or are in the process of implementing CBDCs.

For example, China has been testing its digital yuan since 2014 and has begun rolling it out in certain regions since 2020. The digital yuan is currently being used for everyday transactions in some Chinese cities and is expected to be rolled out nationally in the coming years.

Sweden's central bank, the Riksbank, is also currently testing a CBDC known as the e-krona. The e-krona is being designed to complement physical cash and is currently in the pilot phase.

Other countries that have expressed interest in CBDCs and are exploring their potential implementation include the United States, Canada, the United Kingdom, the Eurozone, Japan, and South Korea.

The rollout of CBDCs has raised concerns about government surveillance and control over financial transactions.

Governor Ron DeSantis proposed a bill to ban CBDCs in Florida.

"The Biden administration's efforts to inject a Centralized Bank Digital Currency is about surveillance and control," he said in a statement, asserting that it "will stifle innovation and promote government-sanctioned surveillance."

South Dakota Governor Kristi Noem vetoed House Bill 1193, a bill which redefined the word money to exclude digital assets and laid the groundwork for a Central Bank Digital Currency (CBDC) as an official state-regulated currency.

Also, Senator Ted Cruz proposed legislation to block a central bank digital currency from being issued in the United States, joining a growing chorus of prominent GOP politicians pushing back against the concept.

But it is not entirely rightists who oppose CBDCs. Several liberal and progressive commentators have spoken out against CBDCs including Jimmy Dore, Russel Brand, and Bret Weinstein. Central Bank Digital Currency is a bipartisan issue. However, Robert F. Kennedy Jr. remains the sole prominent Democrat politician opposing CBDCs.

In a tweet Kennedy stated, "While cash transactions are anonymous, a #CBDC will allow the government to surveil all our private financial affairs. The central bank will have the power to enforce dollar limits on our transactions restricting where you can send money, where you can spend it, and when money expires.

"A CBDC tied to digital ID and social credit score will allow the government to freeze your assets or limit your spending to approved vendors if you fail to comply with arbitrary diktats, i.e. vaccine mandates…

"Watch as governments, which never let a good crisis go to waste, use Covid-19 and the banking crisis to usher in a new wave of CBDCs as a safe haven from germ-laden paper currencies or as protection against bank runs."

Other politicians, such as Senator Elizabeth Warren, a democrat from Massachusetts, express their support for CBDCs. During an appearance on Meet the Press Reports, Warren emphasized, "...let's do a central bank digital currency...I think it's time for us to move in that direction."

Executive order 14067, issued by Joe Biden, addresses digital assets and underscores the need for urgent research and development of a potential United States CBDC, should its issuance be deemed in the national interest.

Central Bank Digital Currencies have the potential to impact individuals' privacy and freedom, depending on their specific design and implementation. CBDCs, as digital currencies issued by a central bank, may enable the government to monitor transactions and potentially gather data on individuals' financial activities. However, it is worth noting that it is possible to design CBDCs that prioritize user privacy, utilizing encryption and anonymization techniques. Nevertheless, without public pressure and scrutiny from third-party experts to assess its acceptability and ethical implications, it is unlikely that the government will prioritize individual freedom if it implements CBDCs.

*Chapter 11*:
Historical Financial Tyranny

Financial tyranny has occurred at points in history where those in power used their control over financial resources to oppress or exploit the masses or certain groups of people. This form of tyranny was often seen in societies where there was a large wealth gap between the ruling class and the common people, and where the ruling class used their wealth to maintain power and control over others.

One example of historical financial tyranny is the system of feudalism that existed in Europe during the Middle Ages. Feudal lords controlled large amounts of land and resources, and the common people were often forced to work for these lords in exchange for protection and basic necessities. This system allowed the lords to accumulate vast amounts of wealth and power, while the common people were often left impoverished and oppressed.

A more extreme and gross abuse of power is the exploitative and dehumanizing institution of slavery, which was prevalent in various regions throughout history, such as ancient Greece, Rome, and the United States during the 18th and 19th centuries. During this time, individuals claimed ownership over slaves and ruthlessly controlled them, unjustly profiting from their labor. This oppressive practice allowed the slave owners to amass wealth and wield power, all at the expense of the enslaved individuals who endured grueling hours of hard labor without fair compensation.

*Financial Confiscation of the People*:

Throughout history, governments have often tried to regulate the possession of gold by its citizens, with some even going so far as to outright ban the possession of the precious metal. This has happened in various countries, at different times, for various reasons. One notable example is the United States' ban on private ownership of gold from 1933 to 1974. Was it moral to obey these bans?

The United States' gold confiscation order of 1933 was issued by President Franklin D. Roosevelt in an attempt to combat the Great Depression. The order required all citizens to turn in their gold coins, bullion, and certificates to the Federal Reserve. Citizens who failed to comply with the order could be fined up to $10,000 and face up to 10 years in prison. The government promised to pay citizens $20.67 per ounce of gold, the then-current price, in exchange for their gold.

Many citizens, however, were reluctant to give up their gold and instead opted to hide it. Some buried their gold in their backyards, while others kept it hidden in their homes. There were also reports of people smuggling gold out of the country to avoid confiscation.

Those who held onto their gold were eventually rewarded for their disobedience. In 1971, President Richard Nixon officially ended the gold standard, allowing gold prices to rise. By 1974, citizens were once again allowed to own gold, and the price had risen to $185 per ounce. Those who had held onto their gold for over 40 years were able to profit handsomely.

The morality of obeying a government ban on gold possession is a complex issue. On one hand, citizens have a duty to obey the laws of their country, even if they disagree with them. Disobeying the law can have serious consequences, including fines, imprisonment, and even death. On the other hand, citizens also have the right to property and to protect their own interests. The government's confiscation of private property, even for a supposedly noble cause like fighting the Great Depression, can be seen as a violation of this right.

The legitimacy of government edicts banning gold possession is a matter of debate. In the case of the United States' gold confiscation order of 1933, it could be argued that the government had the right to regulate gold possession in order to stabilize the economy. However, the order did not give citizens a choice in the matter, and the government did not offer fair compensation for the gold it took. This raises questions about the legitimacy of the order and whether it was truly in the best interests of the country.

Financial tyranny has taken many different forms, but it has always been characterized by the use of financial resources to maintain power and control over the masses. While many societies have moved away from these types of systems, financial oppression and exploitation still exist in many parts of the world today.

## Chapter 12:
### Bitcoin's White Paper

Bitcoin's white paper is a document that was published by Satoshi Nakamoto, the creator of Bitcoin, in 2008. It is a technical paper that outlines the fundamental concepts and principles behind Bitcoin, the world's first decentralized digital currency. The white paper is titled "Bitcoin: A Peer-to-Peer Electronic Cash System" and is considered to be the blueprint for the development of the Bitcoin network.

The white paper describes Bitcoin as a decentralized digital currency that allows for secure, peer-to-peer transactions without the need for a centralized intermediary, such as a bank or financial institution. It introduces the concept of a blockchain, a distributed ledger that records all transactions on the Bitcoin network. The white paper also outlines the process of mining, which is the process of verifying transactions and adding them to the blockchain.

The key innovation of Bitcoin, as described in the white paper, is its use of cryptographic techniques to secure transactions and prevent double-spending. It uses a decentralized network of nodes to verify and validate transactions, which makes it resistant to hacking and fraud.

Overall, the Bitcoin white paper is an important document that has had a profound impact on the development of the cryptocurrency industry. It has inspired the creation of numerous other cryptocurrencies and blockchain-based technologies, and it continues to be a source of inspiration for those working to advance the field of decentralized finance.

Here is the introduction of Bitcoin's White Paper:

## Bitcoin: A Peer-to-Peer Electronic Cash System
### Satoshi Nakamoto

**Abstract.** A purely peer-to-peer version of electronic cash would allow online payments to be sent directly from one party to another without going through a financial institution. Digital signatures provide part of the solution, but the main benefits are lost if a trusted third party is still required to prevent double-spending. We propose a solution to the double-spending problem using a peer-to-peer network. The network timestamps transactions by hashing them into an ongoing chain of hash-based proof-of-work, forming a record that cannot be changed without redoing the proof-of-work. The longest chain not only serves as proof of the sequence of events witnessed, but proof that it came from the largest pool of CPU power. As long as a majority of CPU power is controlled by nodes that are not cooperating to attack the network, they'll generate the longest chain and outpace attackers. The network itself requires minimal structure. Messages are broadcast on a best effort basis, and nodes can leave and rejoin the network at will, accepting the longest proof-of-work chain as proof of what happened while they were gone.

# 1. Introduction

Commerce on the Internet has come to rely almost exclusively on financial institutions serving as trusted third parties to process electronic payments. While the system works well enough for most transactions, it still suffers from the inherent weaknesses of the trust based model. Completely non-reversible transactions are not really possible, since financial institutions cannot avoid mediating disputes. The cost of mediation increases transaction costs, limiting the minimum practical transaction size and cutting off the possibility for small casual transactions, and there is a broader cost in the loss of ability to make non-reversible payments for nonreversible services. With the possibility of reversal, the need for trust spreads. Merchants must be wary of their customers, hassling them for more information than they would otherwise need. A certain percentage of fraud is accepted as unavoidable. These costs and payment uncertainties can be avoided in person by using physical currency, but no mechanism exists to make payments over a communications channel without a trusted party.

What is needed is an electronic payment system based on cryptographic proof instead of trust, allowing any two willing parties to transact directly with each other without the need for a trusted third party. Transactions that are computationally impractical to reverse would protect sellers from fraud, and routine escrow mechanisms could easily be implemented to protect buyers. In this paper, we propose a solution to the double-spending problem using a peer-to-peer distributed timestamp server to generate computational proof of the chronological order of transactions. The system is secure as long as honest nodes collectively control more CPU power than any cooperating group of attacker nodes.

## 2. Transactions

We define an electronic coin as a chain of digital signatures. Each owner transfers the coin to the next by digitally signing a hash of the previous transaction and the public key of the next owner and adding these to the end of the coin. A payee can verify the signatures to verify the chain of ownership.

Read Bitcoin's full white paper here:

https://bitcoin.org/bitcoin.pdf

*Chapter 13*:
Other Promising Cryptocurrencies

### *Ethereum*:

Ethereum is a decentralized, open-source blockchain platform that enables developers to build decentralized applications (dApps) and smart contracts. Ethereum was first proposed in 2013 by Vitalik Buterin, a Russian-Canadian programmer, and was launched in 2015.

Ethereum's native cryptocurrency is Ether (ETH), which is used to pay for transaction fees and computational services on the Ethereum network. Like Bitcoin, Ethereum operates on a decentralized network, which means that there is no central authority controlling the network or its operations.

One of the key features of Ethereum is its ability to execute smart contracts, which are self-executing contracts with the terms of the agreement between buyer and seller being directly written into lines of code. Smart contracts can be used to automate the exchange of assets, such as digital tokens, and can be used to build decentralized applications for a wide range of purposes, from finance to supply chain management to gaming.

Ethereum is also known for its flexibility and programmability, which allows developers to create custom tokens and protocols on top of the Ethereum blockchain. This has led to the creation of a thriving ecosystem of decentralized applications and protocols, with projects ranging from DeFi (decentralized finance) platforms to NFT (non-fungible token) marketplaces to social media networks.

Overall, Ethereum is a powerful blockchain platform that enables developers to create decentralized applications and smart contracts, providing a flexible and programmable foundation for a range of use cases and applications.

***Cosmos:***

Cosmos is a decentralized blockchain platform that aims to create an interoperable ecosystem of independent blockchains. The platform is designed to solve the scalability and interoperability issues faced by many blockchain networks, allowing them to connect and communicate with each other.

The ATOM cryptocurrency is used as the native token of the Cosmos network, serving as the primary means of exchange and transaction settlement within the network. It is used to pay transaction fees, as well as to participate in network governance and decision-making.

One of the key features of the Cosmos network is its Inter-Blockchain Communication (IBC) protocol, which allows different blockchains to communicate and exchange information with each other in a secure and decentralized manner. This allows for the creation of interconnected blockchain networks, known as "zones", that can interact with each other and share data and assets.

The Cosmos platform is also designed to be highly customizable and modular, allowing developers to build and launch their own blockchain applications on the network. This is made possible through the use of the Cosmos

Software Development Kit (SDK), which provides developers with the tools and resources they need to create custom blockchains and decentralized applications (dApps).

Overall, the Cosmos platform and ATOM cryptocurrency aim to provide a decentralized, interoperable, and customizable blockchain ecosystem that can be used by individuals, businesses, and organizations around the world. While the platform is still in its early stages, it has gained a following among blockchain enthusiasts and has been listed on most major cryptocurrency exchanges.

*Kava*:

Kava is a decentralized blockchain platform and cryptocurrency designed to provide a range of financial services, including lending, borrowing, and trading. The platform aims to provide a decentralized alternative to traditional financial institutions, giving users greater control over their finances and eliminating the need for intermediaries.

The Kava platform uses a unique consensus mechanism called "Proof of Stake" to secure the network and validate transactions. This mechanism requires users to hold a certain amount of KAVA tokens to participate in network governance and earn rewards for validating transactions.

One of the main features of the Kava platform is its lending and borrowing functionality, which allows users to borrow and lend cryptocurrencies, including KAVA itself, in a decentralized manner. This functionality is powered by the Kava CDP (Collateralized Debt Position) system, which allows users to borrow stablecoins against their cryptocurrency holdings as collateral.

The KAVA cryptocurrency is used to pay transaction fees on the platform, as well as to participate in network governance and earn rewards for validating transactions. The supply of

Kava is limited to 100 million tokens, with the majority of tokens allocated to the Kava team, investors, and ecosystem development.

Overall, Kava aims to provide a decentralized, secure, and transparent financial platform that can be used by anyone, anywhere in the world. While the platform is still relatively new, it has gained a following among cryptocurrency enthusiasts and has been listed on several major exchanges.

### *Cardano*:

Cardano is a decentralized blockchain platform that was launched in 2017 by Input Output Hong Kong (IOHK), a blockchain research and development company led by Charles Hoskinson, one of the co-founders of Ethereum. Cardano's native cryptocurrency is called ADA.

One of the key features of Cardano is its use of a proof-of-stake (PoS) consensus algorithm, called Ouroboros, which aims to provide a more energy-efficient and secure way of validating transactions on the blockchain. Unlike proof-of-work (PoW) algorithms, which require miners to perform complex mathematical computations to validate transactions, PoS algorithms rely on validators, who hold a stake in the network and are chosen to validate transactions based on the amount of stake they hold.

Cardano is also designed to be scalable and modular, allowing for the development of custom applications and smart contracts on the blockchain. Cardano's development is driven by a research-first approach, with a focus on formal verification, a mathematical method for ensuring the correctness of software and protocols.

Cardano has also put a strong emphasis on governance and community-driven decision-making. The Cardano blockchain includes a built-in governance system, which allows stakeholders to vote on proposals for protocol upgrades and improvements.

Overall, Cardano aims to provide a secure, scalable, and sustainable blockchain platform that can support a wide range of decentralized applications and use cases, from finance to identity management to supply chain management. At time of writing, Cardano is one of the top ten largest cryptocurrencies by market capitalization.

## *Tron*:

Tron (TRX) is a decentralized blockchain platform that was founded in 2017 by Justin Sun, a Chinese entrepreneur and former chief representative of Ripple in China. Tron aims to provide a decentralized platform for content creators to share and monetize their digital content, such as music, videos, and games, without relying on centralized platforms like YouTube or Facebook.

Tron operates on a decentralized network, similar to other blockchain platforms, and uses a proof-of-stake (PoS) consensus algorithm to validate transactions and create new blocks. Tron's native cryptocurrency is called TRX, and it is used to pay for transaction fees and computational services on the Tron network.

One of Tron's key features is its ability to support smart contracts and decentralized applications (dApps) built on the platform. Tron aims to provide a more affordable and scalable alternative to existing blockchain platforms like Ethereum, which has faced challenges with high fees and network congestion.

Tron has also made efforts to establish partnerships and collaborations with various companies and organizations, including BitTorrent, a peer-to-peer file sharing platform that

Tron acquired in 2018, and Samsung, which has included support for Tron dApps on its blockchain-enabled smartphones.

Overall, Tron aims to provide a decentralized platform for content creators and developers to create and share their digital content, while also providing a scalable and affordable alternative to existing blockchain platforms. At time of writing, Tron is one of the top 20 largest cryptocurrencies by market capitalization.

***Stellar Lumens***:

Also known as XLM, Stellar Lumens is a cryptocurrency that is designed to facilitate fast and secure cross-border payments. It was created by Jed McCaleb in 2014, who was also a co-founder of Ripple.

Stellar Lumens uses a decentralized blockchain technology to allow for the transfer of funds between two parties, regardless of their location or currency. The platform works by connecting banks, payment systems, and individuals through a global network, enabling faster and cheaper transactions than traditional banking systems.

One of the key features of Stellar Lumens is its ability to convert between different currencies seamlessly. This is done through the use of a decentralized exchange, which allows users to trade between various currencies without having to go through a centralized exchange. The exchange is powered by the Stellar network's native token, Lumens (XLM).

Stellar Lumens has gained popularity over the years, and its market capitalization has grown significantly since its launch. It is supported by a strong community of developers, contributors, and users who are working to improve the platform and expand its reach.

It's worth noting that while Stellar Lumens and other cryptocurrencies offer exciting possibilities for the future of finance, they are also subject to volatility and risk. As with any investment, it is important to do your own research and assess your own risk tolerance before investing.

*Decentraland*:

Decentraland is a decentralized virtual world built on the Ethereum blockchain. It allows users to create, experience, and monetize content and applications in a 3D virtual space that is owned and controlled by its users.

In Decentraland, users can buy virtual land using MANA, the platform's native cryptocurrency. Once they own land, users can build on it using a variety of tools and programming languages, creating everything from games and virtual art galleries to social clubs and retail spaces.

Decentraland is designed to be entirely user-owned and governed. The platform is controlled by a decentralized autonomous organization (DAO), which is made up of MANA holders who vote on important decisions related to the platform's development and governance.

The platform also features a marketplace where users can buy and sell virtual goods and services using MANA. This includes everything from clothing and accessories to artwork and virtual real estate.

Decentraland has gained popularity in the blockchain and gaming communities due to its unique blend of blockchain technology and virtual world experiences. As the metaverse continues to grow and become more mainstream, it's likely that Decentraland will be at the forefront of this movement, creating new opportunities for users to create and experience immersive virtual experiences.

### *Baby Doge*:

BABYDOGE is a cryptocurrency that was launched in June 2021 as a spinoff of the popular Dogecoin cryptocurrency. BABYDOGE is designed to be a deflationary token, meaning that its supply is limited and will decrease over time, which is intended to increase its value.

According to its website, Baby Doge was created as a "cute and cuddly" version of Dogecoin, with the aim of promoting the use of cryptocurrencies for charitable causes. The Baby Doge team has pledged to donate a portion of each transaction fee to various animal charities and shelters.

BABYDOGE uses a decentralized network, similar to Dogecoin and other cryptocurrencies, and can be bought and sold on various cryptocurrency exchanges. Like other cryptocurrencies, BABYDOGE's value is determined by market demand, and its price can be volatile.

As of early 2022, Baby Doge has gained a significant following on social media, particularly on Twitter and Reddit, with many users promoting the token and sharing memes and artwork featuring the Baby Doge character. However, it is important to note that investing in cryptocurrencies, including BABYDOGE, carries risks, and investors should do their own research and exercise caution before investing.

*Further Examination*:

There are several websites that can be useful for researching different cryptocurrencies, each with their own strengths and weaknesses. Here are a few popular ones:

1.      CoinMarketCap - this website provides information on various cryptocurrencies, including their market capitalization, price, trading volume, and other key metrics.

2.      CoinGecko - similar to CoinMarketCap, CoinGecko provides comprehensive data on cryptocurrencies, including market capitalization, trading volume, and price movements, as well as social media and community activity.

3.      CryptoSlate - this website offers a wide range of cryptocurrency news, analysis, and data, as well as a directory of various blockchain projects and cryptocurrencies.

4.      CryptoCompare - this website provides real-time data on cryptocurrencies, including market capitalization, trading volume, and historical price charts, as well as news and analysis.

5.      Reddit - while not a traditional research website, Reddit can be a valuable resource for learning about different cryptocurrencies and engaging with the community. There are many cryptocurrency-specific subreddits that can provide insights and perspectives from other investors and enthusiasts.

It's important to note that while these websites can provide useful information, they should not be the sole basis for making investment decisions. It's always recommended to conduct your own research and exercise caution before investing in any cryptocurrency.

*Chapter 14*:
BTC Philosophy

At the core of Bitcoin's philosophy is the idea of decentralization, which is rooted in the belief that people should have greater control over their own finances and that governments and financial institutions should not have a monopoly over the monetary system. The idea is that the Bitcoin network is a free-market system that operates independently of any centralized authority, making it more resistant to censorship, corruption, and manipulation.

From a philosophical perspective, Bitcoin aligns with the ideas of libertarianism and Austrian economics. Libertarianism is a political philosophy that emphasizes individual freedom and the minimization of government intervention in people's lives. Austrian economics is a school of thought that emphasizes free markets, property rights, and individual entrepreneurship.

In the context of Bitcoin, these philosophies argue that individuals should have the freedom to transact with each other without interference from a central authority or government. This aligns with the idea that people have the right to their own property and that they should be able to freely exchange goods and services with one another.

Bitcoin also aligns with the philosophy of Friedrich Hayek, a famous Austrian economist who argued that the decentralization of economic power was key to preserving individual freedom. In his book "The Road to Serfdom," Hayek warned against the dangers of central planning and argued that individual economic freedom was essential to maintaining a free society.

Furthermore, Bitcoin's decentralized nature has the potential to disrupt traditional power structures and provide greater financial freedom to individuals in countries with oppressive governments or unstable currencies. This aligns with the philosophy of John Stuart Mill, a British philosopher who argued that individual liberty was essential for personal and societal progress.

However, Bitcoin's libertarian and Austrian economic principles have also been criticized for being overly idealistic and failing to take into account the potential for abuse and exploitation. But the fact remains that every single currency, whether crypto or fiat, carries this risk.

Ultimately, BTC was created as a way for individuals to have complete control over their money and their financial transactions. This is in stark contrast to traditional currency systems, where banks and governments have ultimate control over the flow of money.

*Sound Money and the Rise of Bitcoin:*

In the world of finance and economics, the concept of "sound money" holds great significance. It refers to a monetary system that possesses specific attributes that contribute to its stability, reliability, and ability to retain value over time. The principles underlying sound money have been instrumental in shaping monetary policies throughout history.

The attributes of sound money were articulated by notable economists and thinkers who recognized the importance of establishing a stable monetary system.

One of the earliest proponents of sound money was the classical economist David Ricardo. In the early 19th century, he argued that sound money should possess certain characteristics, including scarcity, durability, divisibility, uniformity, and transportability. These attributes laid the foundation for the philosophy of sound money.

The philosophy of sound money revolves around the belief that a reliable medium of exchange should serve as a store of value over time. It should be resistant to inflation, maintain purchasing power, and foster trust within the financial system. By embodying scarcity, sound money encourages savings, investment, and long-term economic growth. Furthermore, it acts as a bulwark against the arbitrary manipulation of currency by central authorities, safeguarding individual wealth and economic stability.

Bitcoin, the pioneering cryptocurrency introduced in 2009 by an anonymous figure known as Satoshi Nakamoto, has emerged as a revolutionary force challenging traditional notions of sound money.

Bitcoin exhibits several characteristics that align with the attributes of sound money. Firstly, it boasts scarcity. The total supply of bitcoins is fixed at 21 million, with a predictable and predetermined issuance schedule. This predetermined scarcity is achieved through a process called mining, which involves complex computational tasks, making it increasingly difficult to obtain new bitcoins over time.

Secondly, Bitcoin demonstrates durability. As a digital currency, it is not subject to physical wear and tear, and its underlying blockchain technology ensures the immutability and permanence of transactions. Divisibility is also a key feature of Bitcoin, as it can be divided into small units called satoshis, enabling microtransactions and providing flexibility in value transfer.

Uniformity is achieved through the standardization of the Bitcoin protocol, which ensures compatibility and interoperability across different platforms and wallets. Additionally, Bitcoin possesses a high degree of transportability, as it can be transferred across borders quickly and at a relatively low cost compared to traditional forms of money.

However, Bitcoin also faces challenges in fully adhering to the standards of sound money. One critique is its price volatility, which undermines its role as a stable store of value. While Bitcoin's price has experienced significant appreciation over time, it has also undergone sharp fluctuations, leading to concerns about its suitability as a long-term means of exchange.

The advent of Bitcoin has undoubtedly sparked a paradigm shift in the realm of money and finance. While it aligns with several attributes of sound money, such as scarcity, durability, divisibility, uniformity, and transportability, Bitcoin's volatility raises important considerations. One should be cautious before catching FOMO fever when Bitcoin is pushing new highs.

As the concept of sound money evolves, it is essential to critically assess the role of cryptocurrencies like Bitcoin in the broader financial landscape. The ongoing dialogue surrounding the philosophy of sound money and its intersection with the rise of digital currencies provides an opportunity to explore new financial frontiers and reevaluate traditional monetary systems.

Bitcoin's emergence has spurred discussions among economists, policymakers, and technologists about the future of money and the potential benefits and drawbacks of decentralized digital currencies. It has opened avenues for experimentation and innovation in financial technology, paving the way for the development of numerous other cryptocurrencies and blockchain-based projects.

While Bitcoin may not yet fully embody all the attributes of sound money, its disruptive nature and ability to challenge existing financial paradigms have sparked a reexamination of monetary systems as a whole. It has prompted a broader conversation about the role of central banks, the nature of currency, and the potential for decentralized alternatives to traditional monetary frameworks.

As the technology behind cryptocurrencies continues to evolve, efforts are being made to address the shortcomings of Bitcoin and enhance its suitability as a form of sound money.

Innovations such as stablecoins, which are pegged to stable assets like fiat currencies, aim to provide the stability lacking in Bitcoin's price volatility.

Additionally, advancements in blockchain technology are being explored to improve scalability, transaction speed, and energy efficiency, which are critical factors in achieving widespread adoption and acceptance of quality cryptocurrencies as a viable form of sound money.

The journey toward sound money in the digital age is an ongoing process. It requires a careful balance between technological innovation, economic principles, and the needs and expectations of individuals and societies.

Bitcoin's ascent has ignited a profound transformation in our understanding of money and has brought us closer to the realization of sound money principles in the digital realm.

Whether Bitcoin itself ultimately achieves the status of sound money or serves as a catalyst for the development of more refined and robust monetary systems, it has undeniably reshaped the financial landscape. The legacy of Bitcoin lies not only in its potential as a form of currency but also in the discussions and debates it has inspired, paving the way for a more inclusive, transparent, and resilient future of money.

With Bitcoin's influence nourishing the infrastructure of an ever-emerging high-tech era, the pursuit of financial evolution perseveres on an enduring quest, steadfastly illuminating our collective understanding of the intrinsic nature of money.

*produced by:*

# MatrixMav

Navigating the Post-Truth World…
Shining Light on Technocracy & the Transhuman Agenda:
Identity, Sustainability, Pandemia…
Archiving the World's Most Important, Censored News

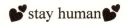 stay human 💔

Diversify your news sources…
Support independent media, & follow **MatrixMav** almost everywhere!
Find us on:

Instagram, Twitter, Facebook, YouTube, Rumble, TikTok, & GETTR:

# @MatrixMav

ISBN:
978-1-312-47183-2